RUGBY
SIMPLIFIED
50 GAMES
FOR SKILL DEVELOPMENT
AND DECISION MAKING

WRITTEN BY CHARLIE PURDON

Contributions by Phil Green and Jake Nelson.
Book design: Jasmine Vowels.

TABLE OF CONTENTS

BALL PRESENTATION + RUCK CLEAN-OUT GAMES

Long body relay

Whirlpool ruck clean-out

Tuisamoa star

Clean-out square

Bear wrestle - square wrestle

Compass

TACKLE TECHNIQUE GAMES

Tracking shoulder bump touch

Rob Du Perez 4 corners chop tackle

Small sided gauntlet/koppe stamp

Keyhole

King of the ring

BALL CARRYING/EVASIVE RUNNING

Simple 1v1 attack games

Cory Jane - stay in field gauntlet

Chaos attack 3v2 - 5v3

4v2 continuous attack for time - 5v3 - 6v4(+2)

5v1 progression counter attack

KICKING

Gainers - gaining grounds

Kicking tennis

Cross-kick - grubber square

Kicking golf

Soccby

Ultimate footy

1. FUN N GAMES

Staying on the theme of, 'Practice the skill, not the drill,' when it comes to fundamental skill development and decision-making. Coaches must create an environment where skills are being practiced in a match simulated situation. This will prepare players to be constantly self-organizing, thinking, and most importantly practice decision making.

Drills can often be monotonous and youth players may not be able to understand the context of the drill or make any kind of relation to the job they'd be tasked with in an actual match. Games or the competition element creates a more dynamic way of learning, HOWEVER these games will only be productive after the skill has been coached correctly. If the fundamental skill is not accurately coached beforehand, then these games may make the player create bad habits through incorrect technique and execution at the expense of winning the game. Winning the game is obviously important but if we focus on the longterm growth and development of each individual, the collective benefits to the team significantly increase our chances of winning. Focus on the processes of performance rather than the outcome/result.

Continue to coach the skill through the game with mantras or key words. Always ask questions to the players at intervals/water breaks to ensure they know why you are playing a specific game and what you are trying to achieve by playing that game. Simple questions such as, what is the most important skill in this game? What is the goal of this game? What have you noticed so far? What has been successful/unsuccessful? What can we do better? Ensure the dialogue is interactive and keep getting as much feedback as possible. Encourage the quieter players to answer questions and always reward effort.

NOTES

_____

_____

_____

People rarely succeed unless they have fun in what they're doing.
- Dale Carnegie

2. WE NOT ME

Always stimulate competition - competition increases productivity and breeds teamwork. Ensure players are always putting effort into a cause far greater than just themselves. Learning to work in a team is not only a great life skill but essential to child's social development. Encourage players to instill strong values into their personal lives that will contribute to their ability to be a good teammate. Players will then bring these positive values into a team environment and assist in building the culture and character of the team.

10 THINGS COACHES LOVE IN A PLAYER:

1 Manners
2 Honesty
3 Respect
4 Character
5 High Work Ethic
6 Fighting Spirit
7 Accountability
8 Coachable
9 Humble
10 Positive Body Language

The onus and responsibility rests on the players. They have a choice between SOAR (Standards Ownership Accountability Responsibility) or BED (Blame Excuses Denial)
- John Mitchell

3. ADAPTIVE TOUCH GAMES:

The games are categorized into adaptive touch games then into 5 core fundamental skills following on from RUGBY SIMPLIFIED - FOR NEW COACHES WITH NO RUCKING CLUE.

1 Catch & Pass - play square
2 Evasive running skills/Ball carrying
3 Tackle technique/completion
4 Breakdown - Ball presentation + Ruck clean out
5 Kicking

A coach must follow the below skills coaching progression before moving onto adaptive games and if necessary refer back to it if bad habits creep back into the games.

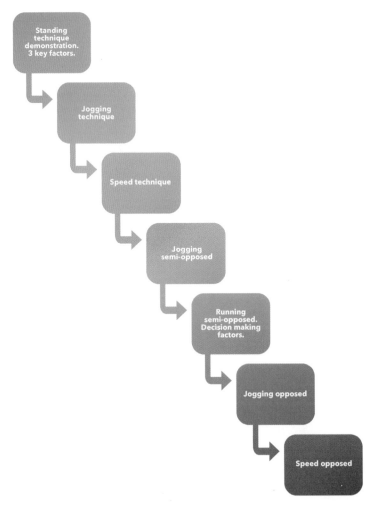

OFFLOAD TOUCH

OBJECTIVE:

To force players to use their agility to evade defenders and GO FORWARD, attempting to get through and behind defensive line. If touched, attacker must look to offload to supporting player in the best possible position to create continuity. Supporting attacking players must work hard off the ball to get in the best possible space to receive the pass.

PRIMARY SKILLS PRACTICED:

Catch Pass, Evasive Running, Continuity, Space Identification, Decision-Making, Support Running Lines - work rate off the ball.

RULES:

- 2 equal teams
- 2 handed touch
- Player touched must turn and offload the ball backwards to teammate
- Unlimited touches
- Upon scoring try, opposition to pick up and attack from try line.
- Defenders must attempt to drop 5m after every touch.

COACHING NOTES:

- Allow touched attacking to turn and continue running backwards with the ball.
- Add time constraint to touched player, i.e. must offload within 3 seconds of being touched.
- Coach must be extremely strict on defensive offside line.
- Must be continuous - team scored on must pick ball up and attack right away.
- Always keep the score.

DENHAM BODY BALL TOUCH

Named after former teammate and friend, Irishman Ian Denham.

OBJECTIVE:

To re-enforce the importance of ball security and ball presentation after the tackle. Once the player is touched he/she must make an aggressive effort to get the ball back efficiently to their own side.

PRIMARY SKILLS PRACTICED:

Ball security, Ball presentation, Catch Pass, Evasive Running, Space identification, Time awareness, Decision-making.

RULES:

- 2 equal teams
- 2 handed touch
- Player touched must secure ball and fight down, recoil body into a long body position and present the ball as efficiently as possible facing own try line.
- Defender whom made touch to attempt to hold attacker off the ground then give resistance to touched player making it difficult to recoil body and present the ball.
- No. of touches at coaches will, recommended 6 touches or unlimited.
- Defense attempt to drop 5m back from line of touch.

COACHING NOTES:

- Ball presentation must be refereed strictly - ball turned over for poor ball security/presentation.
- Ensure attackers are going forward and through the defensive line and not running sideways, to avoid being touched.
- Attackers must be aggressive in their ground fight to ensure accurate ball presentation.

COMBAT ROLL TOUCH

OBJECTIVE:

To force the player to finish over the gain line which will allow for an easier opportunity to present the ball accurately post tackle.

PRIMARY SKILLS PRACTICED:

Ball security, Ball presentation, Catch Pass, Evasive Running, Space identification, Time awareness, Decision-making.

RULES:

- 2 equal teams
- 2 handed touch
- Player touched must secure ball, tumble roll body and recoil into a long body position and present the ball as efficiently as possible facing own try line.
- Unlimited touches.
- Defense attempt to drop 5m back from line of touch.

COACHING NOTES:

- Ball presentation must be refereed strictly - ball turned over for poor ball security/presentation.
- Ensure attackers are going forward and through defensive and not running sideways to avoid being touched.
- Attackers must present the ball with accuracy.

The future belongs to those who learn more skills and combine them in creative ways.

- Robert Greene

RUCK TOUCH → LIVE RUCK

OBJECTIVE:

To force the players to retain possession of the ball through accurate ball presentation and rucking skills, as well as attain the possession through smart, well-timed ball poaching skills.

PRIMARY SKILLS PRACTICED:

Ball security, Ball presentation, Ruck clean out, Catch Pass, Evasive Running, Time and Space awareness, Decision-making.

RULES:

- 2 equal teams
- 2 handed touch
- Player touched must secure ball, go to ground, recoil body into long body position.
- Ruck becomes live after the touch and all regular ruck rules apply.
- Supporting players to clean out potential threat or legally seal off ball from defense.
- Unlimited touches.
- Defense attempt to drop behind last man's feet until ball is out of ruck.

COACHING NOTES:

- Ball presentation must be refereed strictly - ball turned over for poor ball security/presentation.
- Defensive team may poach ball but only within regular rucking laws.
- Ensure attackers are going forward and through defensive and not running sideways to avoid being touched.
- Touched attackers must present the ball with accuracy.

DROP OFF TOUCH

OBJECTIVE:

To create a situation where defenders are always losing players out of the defensive line, giving the attacking team the opportunity to identify areas of the field of defensive vulnerability and scoring opportunities.

PRIMARY SKILLS PRACTICED:

Space identification, Catch Pass, Decision-making, Evasive running, Conditioning.

RULES:

- 2 equal teams
- 2 handed touch
- Player touched must place ball and roll between legs.
- Player who made touched must turn and run back to own try line before returning to play.
- Unlimited touches
- Upon scoring try, opposition to pick up and attack from try line.
- Other defenders must attempt to drop 5m after every touch.

COACHING NOTES:

- Coach must be extremely strict on defensive offside line.
- Must be continuous - team scored on must pick ball up and attack right away.
- Always keep the score.

4 HANDED TOUCH

OBJECTIVE:

To create a connection between defenders and ensure inside and outside defenders of the primary defender (player making the initial touch), are constantly working and making a decision on whether to commit to the attacking player or stay out and ensure appropriate spacing and alignment.

PRIMARY SKILLS PRACTICED:

Catch up defender, Spacing and alignment, Catch Pass, Decision-making, Evasive running, Time/Space awareness.

RULES:

- 2 equal teams
- 2 defenders have to both make a 2 handed touch on attacking player.
- Player touched must place ball and roll between legs.
- Unlimited touches then set constraint - 3 or 6 touches.
- Upon scoring try, opposition to pick up and attack from try line.
- Non-touching defenders must attempt to drop 5m after every touch.

COACHING NOTES:

- Coach must be extremely strict on defensive offside line.
- Must be continuous - team scored on must pick ball up and attack right away.
- Always keep the score.

2 BALL → 3 BALLS

OBJECTIVE:

To get players anticipating ahead and self organizing on attack and defense for what is about to occur in the near or distant future. This also is an excellent conditioning game and a great way to practice fundamental skills under fatigue.

PRIMARY SKILLS PRACTICED:

Conditioning, Self organization, Catch Pass, Decision-making, Evasive running, Time/Space awareness.

RULES:

- 2 equal teams
- 2 or 3 different colored balls.
- Player touched must place ball and roll between legs.
- Unlimited touches or 6 touches.
- Use a different ball every touch, 3rd touch or 6th touch or whenever ref decides.
- Upon change of ball, last player to touch ball must drop it where touched.
- Upon scoring try, opposition to pick up and attack from try line.
- Non-touching defenders must attempt to drop 5m after every touch.

COACHING NOTES:

- Coach must be extremely strict on defensive offside line.
- Coach to consistently communicate throughout the game as to number of touches and which ball to attack from.
- Must be continuous - team scored on must pick ball up and attack right away.
- Always keep the score.

3 PHASES → KICK

OBJECTIVE:

To get players to build a stable platform from which to exit out of their own half and gain territory of the field. This is also a great game to practice building your kick chase line and defensive connection between players. It also gives kickers an opportunity to practice execution in a match simulated environment.

PRIMARY SKILLS PRACTICED:

Game management - building an exit, Kicking - territory game, Chase line - defensive line connection, Catch Pass, Decision-making, Evasive running, Time/Space awareness.

RULES:

- 2 equal teams
- Player touched must place ball and roll between legs.
- 3 touches
- After 3rd touch - ball must be passed back to kicker whom kicks for territory.
- Once ball is kicked, the kicking team to build a stable chase line.
- Team receiving the kick to counter attack and build 3 consistent phases.
- Upon scoring try, opposition to pick up and attack from try line.
- Non-touching defenders must attempt to drop 5m after every touch.

COACHING NOTES:

- Coach must be extremely strict on defensive offside line.
- Coach to ensure every player knows the offside rules from a kick.
- Must be continuous - team scored on must pick ball up and attack right away.
- Always keep the score.

VARIOUS BALLS TOUCH

OBJECTIVE:

To constantly challenge players catching and passing abilities by using various balls of different size and weight. It's a fun game to use to progress the players hand-eye coordination. Scanning with the eyes and concentration are massively important areas of development especially at a beginner/youth level.

PRIMARY SKILLS PRACTICED:

Catch Pass - hand-eye co-ordination, Decision-making, Evasive running, Time/Space awareness, Spacing and alignment.

RULES:

- 2 equal teams
- 3 or more different type of balls. i.e. rugby ball, soccer ball, tennis ball, lacrosse ball, beach ball etc.
- Player touched must place ball and roll between legs.
- Unlimited touches or 6 touches.
- Use a different type of ball every 3 minutes or at coaches will.
- Upon change of ball, last player to touch ball must drop it where touched.
- Upon scoring try, opposition to pick up and attack from try line.
- Non-touching defenders must attempt to drop 5m after every touch.

COACHING NOTES:

- Coach must be extremely strict on defensive offside line.
- Coach to consistently challenge players at times of discomfort/un-organization.
- Must be continuous - team scored on must pick ball up and attack right away.
- Always keep the score.

TOUCH FOOTY - 6 DOWN → 3 DOWN

OBJECTIVE:

To make players attack at a very high tempo and intensity. Defense need to be constantly dropping back onside after every touch. Attacking team must build phases accurately and score within 6 phases. Excellent game to play in order to practice skills under fatigue.

PRIMARY SKILLS PRACTICED:

Catch Pass, High tempo, Evasive running, Continuity, Space identification, Decision-making, Support running lines - work rate off the ball, Conditioning.

RULES:

- 2 equal teams, 6 players per team.
- 1 handed touch
- Player touched must place ball on ground between legs immediately after being touched. Next player to play it - no running scrumhalf - if touched = turnover ball.
- 6 or 3 touches
- Upon scoring try, opposition to start from halfway line.
- Defenders must attempt to drop 5m after every touch.

COACHING NOTES:

- Coach must be extremely strict on defensive offside line.
- Must be continuous - team scored on must pick ball up and attack right away.
- Always keep the score.

GREEN RUCK TOUCH

Named after Australian OMBAC coach Phil Green. A good friend and mentor.

OBJECTIVE:

This game is often used as a conditioning game because of the high work load demanded by the players. It is also a great game for players to practice skills and attacking shape under fatigue.

PRIMARY SKILLS PRACTICED:

Ball security, Ball presentation, Ruck clean out, Catch Pass, Evasive Running, Time and Space awareness, Decision-making.

RULES:

- 3 equal teams - (2 teams play between 22m and opposite try line whilst 1 recovers in the 22m line)
- 2 handed touch
- Play restarts with a kick off from 50m.
- Player touched must secure ball, go to ground, recoil body into long and strong body position.
- Ruck becomes live after the touch and all regular ruck rules apply.
- Supporting players to clean out potential threat or legally seal off ball from defense.
- Unlimited touches. Divide play into 5 - 8min blocks. Team's rotate between attack - defense - active recovery).
- Defense to drop behind last man's feet until ball is out of ruck.

COACHING NOTES:

- Ball presentation must be refereed strictly - ball turned over for poor ball security/presentation.
- Defensive team may poach ball but only within regular breakdown laws.
- Ensure attackers are going forward and through defensive and not running sideways to avoid being touched.
- Touched attackers must present the ball with accuracy.

10-12 V 6 CHAOS DEFENSE TOUCH

OBJECTIVE:

This game is created to deal with match-like situations whereby the defensive team would have less players on their feet than that of their opposition.

PRIMARY SKILLS PRACTICED:

Scramble Defense, Shadow Defense, Catch Pass, Evasive Running, Time and Space Awareness, Decision-Making.

RULES:

- 10 - 12 attackers, 6 defenders
- 40m x 40m field
- 2 handed touch
- Player touched must secure ball, go to ground, recoil body into long body position.
- 1 attack player to seal ruck
- Unlimited touches.
- Defense attempt to drop behind last man's feet until ball is out of ruck.

COACHING NOTES:

- Defense to play soft - down on numbers - shadow defense
- Stern on defensive team's communication and ability to connect
- Ball presentation must be refereed strictly - ball turned over for poor ball security/presentation.
- Touched attackers must present the ball with accuracy.

Get comfortable with being uncomfortable all the time.

- Vern Gambetta

RUCK FRINGE TOUCH

OBJECTIVE:

To force players to use the space on the fringe of the rucks to attack. Getting players looking up and making use of the near space around the breakdown.

PRIMARY SKILLS PRACTICED:

Space identification, Catch Pass, Decision-making, Evasive running, Conditioning.

RULES:

- 2 equal teams
- 2 handed touch
- Player touched must go to ground, recoil body into long body shape ball presentation.
- 1 attacking support player over the ball
- Defender who made the touch and nearest defender to drop to ground and do 5 push ups.
- Unlimited touches
- Upon scoring try, opposition to pick up and attack from try line.
- Other defenders must attempt to drop 5m after every touch.

COACHING NOTES:

- Coach must be extremely strict on defensive offside line.
- Players to be disciplined on push ups after the touch before rejoining play.
- Must be continuous - team scored on must pick ball up and attack right away.
- Always keep the score.

CATCH PASS GAMES:
ULTIMATE PASS BALL $\rightarrow$ VARIOUS BALLS $\rightarrow$ TIME CONSTRAINTS

OBJECTIVE:

Similar to Ultimate Frisbee but obviously replacing the frisbee with a rugby ball. The aim of the game is to compile as many passes as possible as a team without losing possession of the ball through dropped ball, poor pass, or interception by opposition team.

It may seem as though this game has no relevance to the game of rugby however there are a ton of skills being practiced by creating a chaotic environment where a variety of passes are used. The more common skills executed include: Catch Pass, Space identification, Decision-making, Evasive running, Work rate off the ball - Conditioning.

RULES:

- 2 equal teams, No more than 8 players per team.
- Ball hitting ground brings a turnover of possession.
- Defending team not allowed to make contact with attacking players.
- Any type of pass allowed and in any direction desired.
- Create a playing area big enough to cater for space to move into open space, (no smaller than 20x20 yards).

COACHING NOTES:

- Coach must count no. of passes and ensure that the game is continuous and high tempo. Encourage work rate off the ball. Create a constraint - no longer more than 3 seconds with the ball in hand and switch up balls at will, i.e. soccer ball, football, tennis ball etc.

END BALL → PASS BALL W END ZONE

OBJECTIVE:

Basically ultimate pass ball with an end zone/area in which to score points. You can create an end zone line/marked out box in which to score.

RULES:

- The same rules apply as Ultimate Pass Ball but coach must create an area of space/goal-line which to get the ball over to score points, i.e. Ball passed into the end zone/scoring box and caught successfully = 1 point

COACHING NOTES:

- Create a constraint - no longer more than 3 seconds with the ball in hand. Possibly allocate points for kicking the ball successfully into in goal area. Must be continuous and high tempo. Encourage work rate off the ball. Always reward effort and decision-making. Coach always keep the score.

DOC'S GAME

OBJECTIVE:

Named after Dr. Danie Craven, a South African rugby revolutionary in the mid 1900's known for his many quirky and controversial statements and out of the ordinary coaching methods. He was a very successful player, coach and administrator and was inducted into the International Rugby Hall of Fame in 1997. A statue of Doc still stands at Stellenbosch University to this day. He was also first recorded player to ever perform a 'dive pass'.

Doc's game similar to End Ball needs to be played on a full size field with goal posts on each end. The aim of this game is for a team of players to collectively move the ball up field in anyway the player's desire. A point is awarded when the ball is successfully kicked or passed through the goal posts and above the cross bar. The possession is turned over if the ball hits the ground or if a player is touched by an opposition player.

This more than anything can be used as a conditioning game because of the amount of distance each player should cover over the duration of the game.

RULES:

- 2 equal teams, Max 20 players per team.
- Ball hitting ground brings a turnover of possession or if player is touched by opposition player.
- Any type of pass or kick is allowed and in any direction desired.
- Create a playing area big enough to cater for space to move into op
- Points allocation is made at coaches preference

COACHING NOTES:

- Create a constraint if necessary - no longer more than 3-5 seconds with the ball in hand. Must be continuous and high tempo. Encourage work rate off the ball. Always reward effort and decision-making. Coach always keep the score.

SBW OFFLOAD GAUNTLET

OBJECTIVE:

Named after iconic multi sport athlete Sonny Bill Williams. The King of the offload. Similar rules to pass ball apply but defenders will be with contact/ruck shields in hands. The aim of this game is for the attacking players to offload the ball to each other as many times as possible without losing control of the ball or get knocked out of the gauntlet by a defender.

The main principle at focus is ball security and protection. Ensure players are able to maintain a low, strong body position and keep the ball safely for long periods of time.

RULES:

- 2 equal teams, No more than 8 players per team.
- Ball hitting ground/player losing control of ball brings an end to play.
- Defending team allowed to knock attacking player out of gauntlet with tackle shield.
- Any type of pass/offload allowed and in any direction desired.
- Create a small playing area in order for attacking team to maintain ball security and strong body positioning.

COACHING NOTES:

- Coach must be count no. of offloads. Create a time constraint/no. of possessions before turning over possession to opposition team. Encourage work rate off the ball. Support players to get themselves into good areas to receive the ball. Always reward effort and decision-making. Always keep the score.

CHAOS ATTACK - CONTINUOUS 2V1 → 3V2

OBJECTIVE:

The aim of chaos attack is to promote accurate decision making in an environment of high stress like that of a match.

CONTINUOUS 2V1:

Create a square with 4 cones. Divide the attackers between the 4 cones facing each other. Put one defender in the middle of the square. 2 attackers v 1 defender, once through, the player with the ball pops it to the next pair of attackers to attack the single defender. If an attacking player gets touched/drops pass/makes a forward pass then he/she becomes the defender.

RULES:

- Defender may not slap down the pass from one attacker to the next.
- Coach to be the judge of all touches, poor pass.
- Defender to turn immediately and defend the opposition direction.

COACHING NOTES:

- Always reward effort and decision-making. Always promote continuity and high tempo.

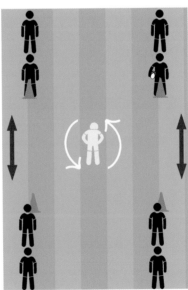

CONTINUOUS 3V2:

OBJECTIVE:

Create a square with 6 cones. Divide the attackers between the 6 cones facing each other. Put 2 defenders in the middle of the square. 3 attackers v 2 defenders, once through, the player with the ball pops it to one of the next trio of attackers to attack the 2 defender. Change the 2 defenders at coaches preference.

RULES:

- Defender may not slap down the pass from one attacker to the next.
- Coach to be the judge of all touches, poor pass.
- Defender to turn immediately and defend the opposition direction.

COACHING NOTES:

- Always reward effort and decision-making. Always promote continuity and high tempo.

SQUARE SPEED PASSING → VARIOUS DISTANCE

RULES:

- Create two lines of 4-6 markers parallel to one another, (depending on no. of players available).
- Start with markers 6yd apart with a player on each marker in groups of 4-6 players.
- Each group of players with a ball starting on one end. Slowly progress the passing lines from walking to jogging and then into running and passing at top speed in the quickest possible time.
- Coach to have a stopwatch and announce the time after each groups effort.
- Players to keep changing position in the line.
- Coach must keep changing direction to which group is passing. Adjust distance between cones when comfortable. Change type of ball to test players choice of pass, i.e. Weighted pass developer ball, Soccer ball, Tennis ball etc.

COACHING NOTES:

- Coach to be strict of technical fundamentals. Use mantra's such as, Hands up, Catch ball early, Hands always above hips, Stay square, Follow through, Complete the pass. Coach to announce the time after every group of passes.

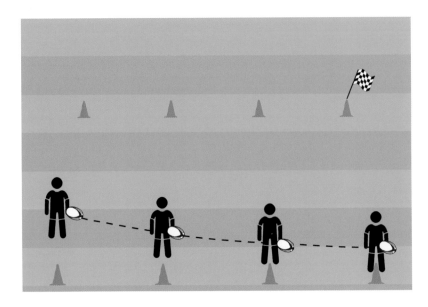

DOUBLE BALL OFFLOAD TOUCH →
EVERYONE WITH BALL IN TWO HANDS

OBJECTIVE:

The aim of this game is to force players to use their agility to evade defenders and GO FORWARD, attempting to get through and behind defensive line. Attacking player to put emphasis on ball security as he/she will have 2 balls on them. If touched, attacker must offload 1 of the 2 balls in player's hands to support player in best possible position to create continuity. Supporting attacking players must work hard off the ball to get in the best possible space to receive the pass.

Ensure each attacking player has 1 ball in their hands. Then begin by player walking touch rugby with the game ball. Once Attacking player is touched, he/she offloads 1 of the 2 balls in his hands to fellow attacking player.

RULES:

- 2 equal teams
- 2 handed touch
- Player touched must turn and offload the ball backwards to teammate.
- Unlimited touches or 10 touches/time constraint
- Defenders must attempt to drop 5m after every touch.

COACHING NOTES:

- Allow touched attacking to turn and continue walking/jogging/running backwards with the ball. Add time constraint to touched player, i.e. must offload within 3 seconds of being touched. Coach must be extremely strict on defensive offside line. After certain period time - change possession over to opposite team. Always keep the score.

3V2 VARIATIONS

ELLA:

OBJECTIVE:

The aim of this game is to create a unstructured shape of defense for players to attack against simulating a chaotic scenario much like in an actual match. Players to individually to keep score of their results on attack. Player with most successive scores is the winner. Players to take turns on attack and defense. Coach to ensure the same 3 attackers aren't attacking together as a team every time.

RULES:

- Create a rectangle with 4 different colored markers parallel to each other.
- Put 3 attackers at one side of the rectangle and 2 defenders at the other end of the rectangle.
- Coach will call two colors for which the 2 defenders must station themselves.
- On the coaches call, 3 attackers will attack up the rectangle vs the 2 defenders coming from different angles.

WESTS:

OBJECTIVE:

Similar to that of the Ella attack game, the aim is to create a chaotic scenario for the attack by having defenders starting at different positions in the grid.

RULES:

- Put out various colored markers up a rectangular grid.
- Place a scrumhalf on the side of one end of the rectangle with 3 attackers.
- Put a defender on every cone.
- The coach will then call 2 colors - the 3 attackers taking a pass from 9 will attack vs two announced defenders up the grid.

KINGS:

RULES:

- Create a mid field ruck with a scrum half.
- Split the group into 3 groups of 4 attackers.
- At all times, you'll have 4 attackers on either side of the ruck and 3 defenders, (1 member of group will sit out when that group is on defense).
- 9 will then pass to attacking group of 4 to attack against 3 defenders.
- Attacking group to attempt to make a line break and score off first phase.
- The 3 groups will then move around in a clockwise direction into the next task.
- Players to take turns on attack and defense. Coach to ensure the same 3 attackers aren't attacking together as a team every time.

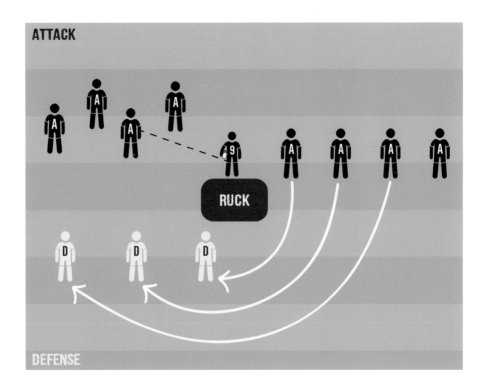

BALL PRESENTATION + RUCK CLEAN-OUT GAMES:

Players need to be made aware of the importance of the breakdown and the retention of possession. Being able to control this area of the game will put opponents under a lot of pressure which will lead to points and ultimately the desirable results. Ensure the players understand all of the breakdown laws and the various referee interpretations in this area of the game.

LONG BODY RELAY

RULES:

- Divide group of players in teams of 6 or 8, with 1 ball for each team.
- Have them lay down on on belly's top to toe in a line. Ball starting at one end.
- Player at start of line to recoil body around on the ground to face teammate whom repeats the action until all players are facing same direction then back towards starting direction.
- Team to get it successfully from one end to the next without losing control of the ball wins.

COACHING NOTES:

- Coach to be strict on recoil technique and ball security + presentation. Repeat until satisfied with presentation quality. Always keep the score.

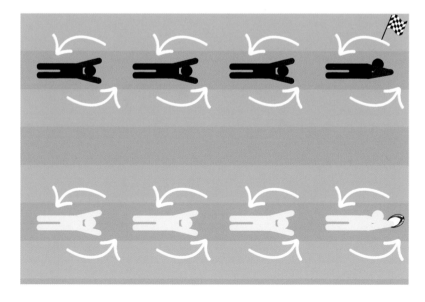

WHIRLPOOL RUCK CLEAN-OUT

OBJECTIVE:

This is a chaos ruck clean-out scenario created by the constraint of players having to move around in a circular motion making it difficult to work back and into breakdown at a legal angle.

RULES:

- Put 4 players in middle of circle with contact shields.
- The rest of the group on the outskirts of the circle.
- Coach to give direction in which the players are to run around (clock-wise or anti-clockwise).
- Coach in the middle of the circle to throw the ball to one attacking player - that attacking player to carry the ball into nearest contact shield. The 3 players supporting players to square up to come through the gate. 2 players to blast and clear out nearest threat, 3rd player to straddle over the ball with eyes up, core on in a strong low body position.
- Coach to judge accuracy of each breakdown and give score out of 10. Players then get up and continue joining the circle in a whirlpool motion.

COACHING NOTES:

- Be strict of recoil technique and ball security + presentation. Repeat until satisfied with presentation quality. Always keep the score.

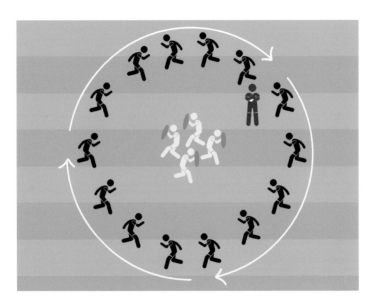

TUISAMOA STAR

OBJECTIVE:

Named after legendary USA Eagle and OMBAC Rugby stalwart and a good friend, Tai Tuisamoa.

RULES:

- 1 player on contact shield, 4 players spread between 4 markers in the shape of a cross.
- Coach to throw the ball to chosen player. Player to then carry the ball into contact shield.
- 3 other players to work around and enter the gate at a legal angle - first 2 players to blast immediate threat, 3rd player to seal over the ball.
- Coach to rank each breakdown on a score out of 10.

COACHING NOTES:

- Be strict of recoil technique and ball security + presentation. Repeat until satisfied with presentation quality. Always keep the score.

CLEAN-OUT SQUARE $\longrightarrow$ 4 BAGS

RULES:

- Create a square with 4 cylinder-shaped take bags. Put a player on each of the 4 tackle bags.
- One player in the middle of the square to clean out all 4 players laying on the tackle bags with different body shapes as to simulate an opposition player at the breakdown.
- Player cleaning out to perform 8 consecutive clean-outs. Coach to judge and score out of 10 on each specific clean-out.

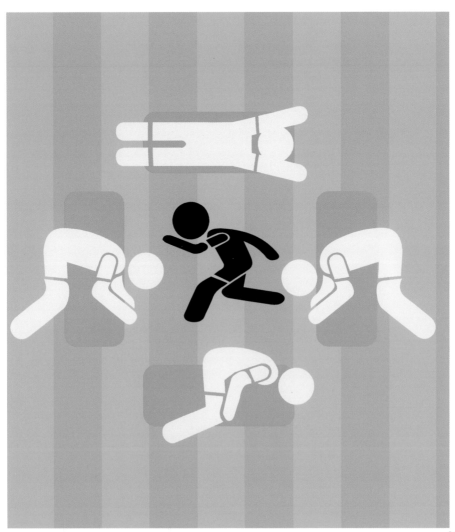

BEAR WRESTLE → SQUAT WRESTLE

RULES:

- Divide players into pairs. Starting on their knees facing each other.
- On coach's call players to wrestle each other and attempt to get opponent down and flat on his back.
- This could then progress into standing and doing the same.
- Coach to put a time constraint i.e. 30 seconds on/ off for 6 rounds. Players to keep score.

- You could create a playoff, 'winner takes all scenario' to see who would be your team's Wrestlemania champion.

COACHING NOTES:

- Ensure high quality. This can be used as a conditioning contact exercise. Always reward effort.

Stringer may as well be looking for a Mars bar in a bucket of shit.

Former Irish coach Eddie O'Sullivan critiquing the forwards rucking style during a training session.

COMPASS

OBJECTIVE:

This breakdown game is also an excellent game to use as a contact conditioning exercise.

RULES:

- Create a large square.
- Put 4 attackers on each side of the square and 3 defenders in the middle of the square.
- Give each side of the square a name preferably, North, South, West, East. On the coaches call, the side he calls out attacks vs the 3 defenders in the middle of the square.
- The attacking team, if tackled, then work back and around to secure that ruck with the non ball-carrying 3 players. That attacking team then stays on the side in which they were attacking. The 3 defenders then get back to their feet and defend the side the coach calls next.
- Add a time constraint of 90 seconds per defending team. The most successful defending team of 3 is the winner.

COACHING NOTES:

- Ensure the timing of this game is selected carefully and according to your season practice session breakdown because of the physical demand placed on the players.

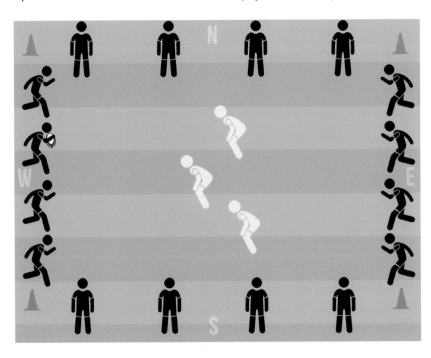

TACKLE TECHNIQUE GAMES:

The tackle is often one of the most difficult skills to teach to new players. Not only for the intricacies of good, safe technique but more from a confidence point of view. Being able to make a tackle is a courageous act. New players often tend to shy away tackling practice from a fear perspective. It's important to recognize and understand this, and ensure the player is able to learn and progress at a rate that he/she is most comfortable with.

An idea for new rugby players is to practice contact work on the beach or in a sandpit. A lot of new players are often very hesitant when it comes to practicing the tackle. You as a coach need to ensure that the player is able to progress at rate most comfortable for his/her personal development.

TRACKING SHOULDER BUMP TOUCH → HANDS BEHIND BACK

OBJECTIVE:

This is an excellent game to re-enforce that a player needs to make shoulder contact first. The constraints are placed in order to correct the tracking and footwork approach to the tackle, more than the actual tackle technique itself. Defenders hands must remain behind back at all times - keep their eyes up, core on and maintain a good low body position when making a 'bump touch'.

RULES:

- 2 equal teams, (no more than 6 per side).
- Defenders with hands behind their backs. Attackers to start with walking touch rugby.
- Touch is called when defender makes shoulder contact with attacker. Defenders hands to remain behind back at all times.

COACHING NOTES:

- Ensure defenders are communicating in a concise and effective manner to each other throughout the game. Make certain defenders are getting their head safely out of the way of the attacker and their eyes stay up the entire time.

ROB DU PREEZ 4 CORNERS CHOP TACKLE

OBJECTIVE:

Named after a personal former coach and current Sharks Super Rugby Head Coach.

RULES:

- Create a square using 4 markers.
- Put 2 players behind each marker facing each other, each given a no. 1-8.
- Put 1 tackler in the middle of the square.
  Players on marker must run diagonally to opposite marker.
  Tackler in middle of square must complete 8 low leg, 'chop' tackles.

COACHING NOTES:

- Coach to judge how many 'chop' tackle completions are made by each tackler.

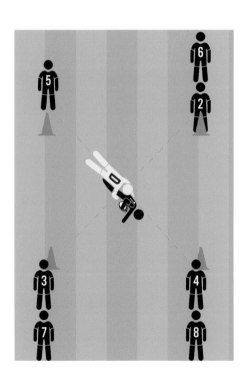

SMALL SIDED TACKLE GAUNTLET/KOPPE STAMP

OBJECTIVE:

This contact game is a staple to every South African youth coach, often played in the in-goal area of the rugby field. It's not only infamous for it's Afrikaans name, (translated to english, Stamp on head) but also encourages a different style of play suited to physically abrasive and aggressive players which is most common in South African teams. It consists of using pure brute force to break opponents down physically opposed to manipulating space through clever deception and swift ball distribution. However way one see's it, this game is simple and has advantages to teaching players the correct tackle technique and close contact skills. Playing this game in a small space and in a controlled environment with constraints will allow a player to gradually build confidence in their ability to make effective and consistent tackle completions.

RULES:

- Create a small field 10yd x 16yd.
- Allocate players into small sided team's, 5-8 players per team - no set-piece's.
- All regular rugby rules apply. Extend field size at coaches preference. Team with the most tries at the end of the allotted time period is the winner.

If you gonna be dumb, you gotta be tough.

- Roger Alan Wade

KEYHOLE

OBJECTIVE:

The aim of this game is to practice tackle completion with the defender approaching the attacker from different angles.

RULES:

- Place a marker at which the attacker is stationed.
- Place 4 different markers around 5 to 10 meters away.
- Put a defender between the 4 various colored cones.
- Coach will then call a color - defender to touch the cone then turn and make a tackle on attacker.
- Coach to counter no. of complete tackles. Player with most accurate completions is the winner.

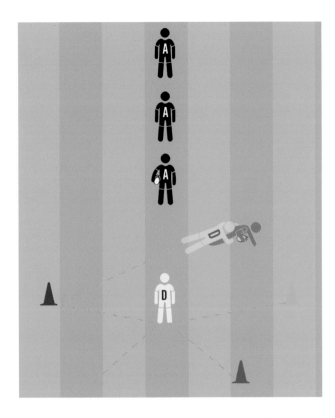

KING OF THE RING

OBJECTIVE:

The aim of this game is practice tackling within a defensive line. A lot of emphasis must be placed on communication. This game could use be used as a way to practice double hits where one player could go low and the other going high attempting to wrap up the ball and hold the attacker up.

RULES:

- 1 attacker in the middle of the circle.
- Defenders form a ring around the attacking player.
- Attacker has 1 min to try get out of the ring.
- Counterintuitively, the attacker that is able to get out of the ring is the winner.

COACHING NOTES:

- An idea for new rugby players is to practice contact work on the beach or in a sandpit. A lot of new players are often very hesitant when it comes to practicing the tackle. You as a coach needs to ensure the player is able to progress at rate comfortable for his/her development.

BALL CARRYING-EVASIVE RUNNING GAMES:

Always ensure that every player in your group is equipped with the necessary skills to evade a defender, preferably through footwork and deception. This skill is not only necessary for the lighter, more shiftier players but also for bigger heavier guys who need to use their agility when carrying ball to get behind the defender - if a player is able to achieve this then it will allow them a better opportunity in which to offload and create continuity off that carry.

SIMPLE 1V1 ATTACKING GAMES

1 Put players in pairs with 1 ball between them. Defending player to place ball on ground and immediately start back tracking. Attacker to pick the ball up and use footwork to turn the defender running backwards and beat him 1v1 with a sidestep.

2 Put players in pairs with 1 ball between them. Create a square, (15 width). Both players on inside edge of the square. Defending player passes to attacker. Attacker to attempt to beat defender.

3 Create a small square with 4 markers, (8yd x 8yd). Put 1 player diagonally across from each other. Attacking player receives a pass from outside the square then attempts to evade defender and score on 1 of two try lines.

4 Split players in two groups lined up in a single file each behind a marker. Put two markers halfway between the two groups. Attacker to evade defender and score behind line. Defender to press up and defend him.

5 Create a triangle with 3 markers. Attacker, (with ball in hand) and defender to start on same marker. On the coaches call. Players to run around respectful markers. Attacker to attempt to evade defender in a (15 to 25 yards of width).

6 Put two groups of attackers in a single file on either side, both facing the defender. Attacker to evade single defender then offload the ball to attacker on opposite side who attacks the same defender. Defender to keep defending for a set duration of time, (i.e, 90 secs).

SIMPLE 1V1 ATTACKING GAMES #2

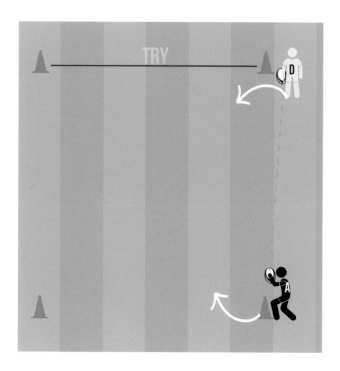

SIMPLE 1V1 ATTACKING GAMES #3

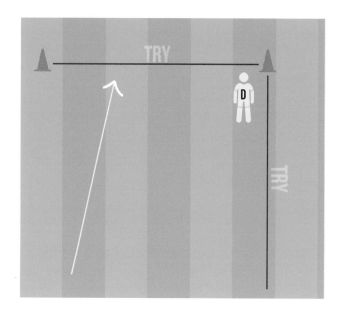

SIMPLE 1V1 ATTACKING GAMES #4

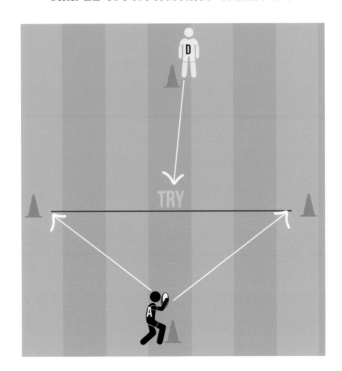

SIMPLE 1V1 ATTACKING GAMES #5

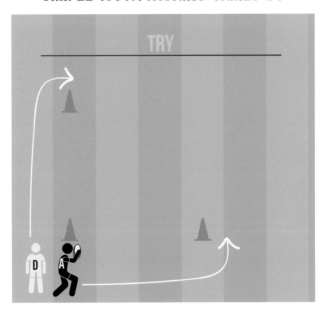

CORY JANE-STAY IN-FIELD GAUNTLET
→ 2V1 GAUNTLET

Named after former Hurricanes and All Black winger, Cory Jane whom possessed an iconic hand off and an ability to stay in field of play when attacking down the touchline.

Set out a corridor along the 5m line and outline with cones about 25 yards long. Place 5 defenders along the channel/gauntlet each armed with a contact shield. Attacker must run through channel and not get knocked out of the channel by defenders.

The coach could then add a second attacker, 2v1 attack along the channel with the ball carrier getting knocked out of the field of play.

CHAOS ATTACK 3V2 $\longrightarrow$ 5V3

Create a square box. Place 3 cones on each end facing each other. 2 defenders in the middle of the box. 3v2 the pop ball to next set of 3 attackers attacking 3v2 the opposite way. Defenders to turn and defend the opposite way. Coach to change out the 2 defenders every couple of minutes.

4V2 CONTINUOUS ATTACK FOR TIME $\longrightarrow$ 5V3 6V4(+2)

Create a square box with 4 markers. Put 4 attackers on two sides of the square facing each other. Nominate 2 defenders to stay in the middle of the square. 4 attackers to attack vs the 2 defenders. Once through, attackers offload the ball to the next 4 attackers whom attack right away. 2 defenders to turn and defend the opposite side right away.

5V1 PROGRESSION COUNTER ATTACK GAME

This is an outstanding game to practice counter attack from a kicked ball. It forces the attacking team to make good decisions in order to maintain possession of the ball and build phases. It's also a good way for defenders to practice defending an overlap of attacking numbers.

RULES:

- Make 2 teams of 5 players.
- Played on a regular width of rugby field.
- Attacking team spread out along 50m line.
- Ball to be kicked onto attacking team.
- Defending team sends out 1 defender, 5v1 - attackers have 1 phase in which to score. If successful ball gets kicked on to attacking team, defenders send out 2 defenders. Attack has 2 phases in which to score. If successful, 5v3 defenders - 3 phases. 5v4 defenders - 4 phases, 5v5 defenders - 5 phases. If attacking team scores on 5v5, they are then awarded 1 point and continue attacking. If attack makes mistake or is unsuccessful then defensive then becomes attack and attack to defense.

KICKING GAMES:

You may assume that kicking is not an important area of the game to practice at a youth or beginner level however what is important is that new players learn the correct kicking technique as soon as possible before bad habits creep in from other sports.

The rugby ball is a different shape, size, weight and texture than similar shaped balls from other sports and new players need to be taught the correct way to drop it and where on the foot to actually place it.

In kicking games, players are not only practicing their kicking but also catching the ball out of the air and from different angles. What's been quite clearly evident in my career as a coach is the amount of joy a player receives from kicking a ball. Kicking games are a great morale booster for any team and must be played and enjoyed by every member of playing squad regardless of their position.

GAINERS-GAINING GROUNDS GAME:

Players generally divided into even teams with no more than six players per team. Game is played over a full sized rugby field/as bigger a space as possible.

The aim of the game is to kick the ball between the posts for points/over the goal line for points.

RULES:

- The game is started with a drop kick.
- If a player catches the ball directly out of the air, then he/she gets to take 10 steps forward before kicking the ball back.
- If the kick lands in space and rolls, then the opponent must take the return from where the ball stopped rolling or where the player was able to retrieve the ball from.
- Allocate points for
  A). Being able to kick the ball through the posts, and
  B). Being able to kick the ball over the goal-line. The team with the most points at the end of the allotted time is the winner.

KICKING TENNIS:

Divide an area of space into two boxes separated by a 'net'. The space of the 'court' should depend on the number of players in each team.

The aim of the game is to land the ball on the surface of the opponents court. If successful, closest player to the ball is eliminated from the game.

If a player drops the ball attempting to catch it, then he/she is eliminated from the game. If a player gets the ball out of the bounds then he/she is eliminated. The team that ends up with zero players left on the court is the loser.

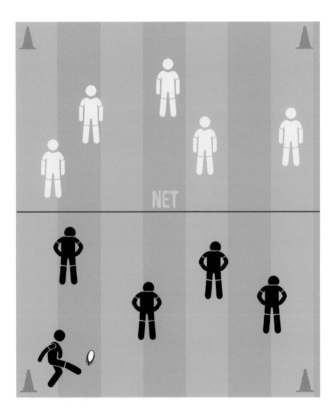

CROSS-KICK → GRUBBER SQUARE:

Divide players up on all 4 corners of a rectangle of space. Players kick diagonally across the rectangle for player stationed on parallel corner of rectangle. Select choice of cross kick, (punt or grubber preferably). Coach must create a point system for good/poor kick. At the end of the allotted time, the player with the highest/lowest score is the winner.

I suggest creating a deficit word point system, i.e. DONKEY. Every time a player kicks a poor kick/drops a ball he/she gets a letter. First person to DONKEY is the loser or is out until the last man is standing/is the winner.

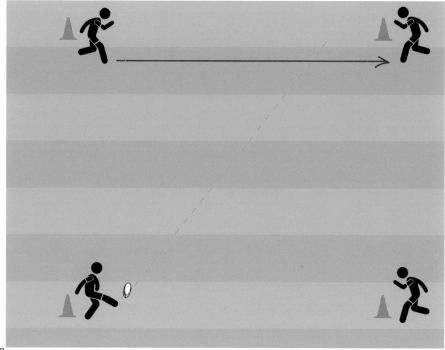

KICKING GOLF

Every player has his own ball or teams of 2 or 3 taking alternating kicks. Choose a marker to use as 'the hole'. Set up a creative course over a large area of space. Player with the least number of kicks at the end of the agreed round of holes is the winner.

SOCCBY

Divide players into 2 teams to play a game of soccer in a marked out field, (with a soccer ball). Players are allowed to kick/scoop the ball with their feet into teammates hands. Once a player is able to achieve this, the game then turns into regular touch rugby. Once player is touch, opposition then start the game of by playing soccer again until the ball is kicked up into players hands. Points should be allocated for either kicking the ball through marked out goal posts/running the ball in for a try over the try line. Team with the most points at the end of the allotted time is the winner.

ULTIMATE FOOTY

Adapted from Australian Rules Football aka Aussie Footy - Ultimate Footy goes by the same principles as ultimate frisbee however the ball, not frisbee, is kicked between players to move the ball down field to marked out goal area. Players may make use any type of kick to distribute the ball between each other. Points are allocated for the number of successfully consecutive kicks between players, in which case the team with the most amount of successful completed kicks is the winner or by kicking the ball between the goal posts, in which case the team with the most combined points is the winner.

PLAY DESIGN BOARD

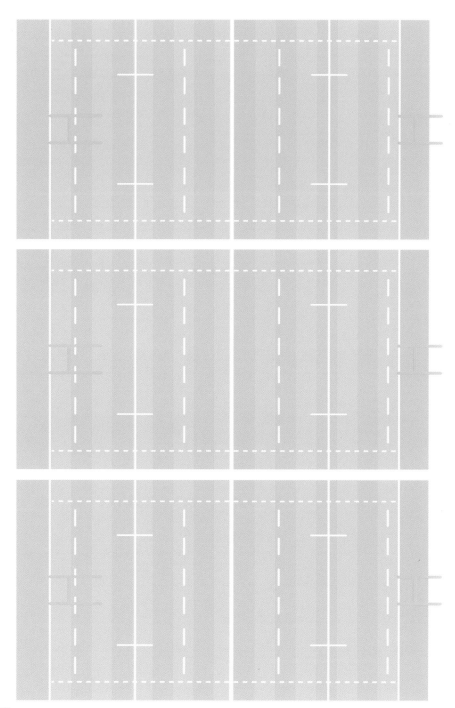

PLAY DESIGN BOARD

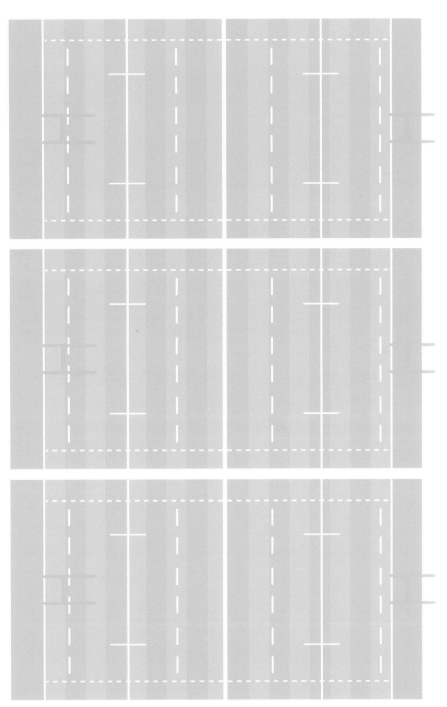

Printed in Great Britain
by Amazon